Contents

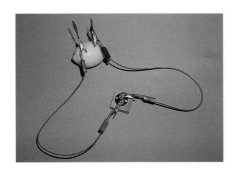

D1429151

Lightning is a source of electrical energy produced during thunderstorms.

Moving objects have movement energy. When the bullet hit the egg its movement energy was transferred to the egg, causing it to explode.

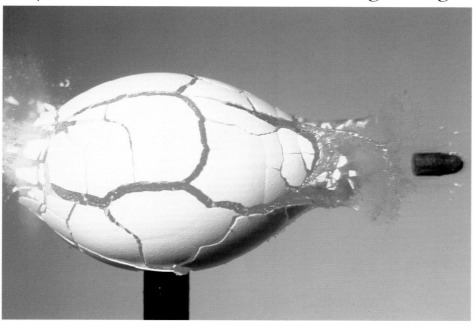

Introduction

All life needs energy. We need energy to move, to grow, to breathe and to reproduce. There are many forms of energy – chemical, heat, light and sound energy. All these forms have one thing in common: energy can do work and it can make something happen. This could be moving something, heating it up or changing it.

Energy is not a substance. You cannot touch energy. But you can see what it does. Imagine that you are making a catapult with an elastic band. You stretch the elastic band. Now the band is ready to do some work. It has potential energy. When you release the band it snaps to its original length. The stored potential energy has been changed to movement energy. This produces a force that is strong enough to hurl a stone forwards at great speed. If the moving stone hits a window it transfers its energy to the glass, causing it to break. The further the elastic band is stretched the more potential energy that can be stored. This means more work can be done when the elastic band is released.

Measuring energy

 *A 16-year-old girl needs
to eat about 9 million
joules of energy each
day. A 16-year-old boy
needs to eat about 12
million joules.*

Energy can be measured in units called joules.
Packets of food usually have labels which tell
you how much energy is locked up in the
food. The value will be shown either as J
(joules) or kJ (kilojoules), which are thousands
of joules.

The sun is the source of most of the energy
on Earth. This energy comes from the nuclear
reactions taking place in the sun. But the sun is
not a limitless source of energy and one day it
will stop shining altogether. Fortunately this will
not happen for millions of years.

This book looks at the ways in which
energy can be used, captured and changed. It
shows the ways that living organisms use
energy in their lives. Important words are
explained under the heading of **Key words**
and in the glossary on page 44. You will find
some amazing facts in each section, together
with some experiments for you to try and
some questions to think about.

Food contains
chemical
energy. The
food is broken
down and the
energy released.
Then it can be
changed into
other forms of
energy needed
by our bodies.

Key words
Chemical energy the
energy stored in the
chemical bonds of
molecules.
Movement energy the
energy possessed by a
moving object.
Potential energy the
energy stored by an
object.

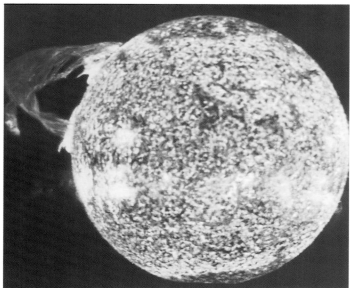

The sun is like a huge nuclear reactor releasing heat and light energy.

 The sun provides most of our heat. Temperatures at the centre of the sun reach a staggering 14,000,000 °C

Heat energy

Heat is the energy of moving molecules. When you heat an object its molecules move faster. The faster the molecules move the hotter that object becomes. The temperature of the object tells us how hot it is. So a thermometer is really measuring how fast the molecules are moving.

If an object is hot it will pass its heat to its surroundings. The surroundings warm up while the object cools down. The transfer of heat can occur in different ways. When you stir a hot drink with a metal spoon it quickly becomes warm. This is heat conduction. A radiator will heat a room by convection. When you sit in front of an open fire you are warmed by heat radiation.

Conduction

When something is heated the molecules within it start to move or vibrate and they bump into each other. They transfer their heat energy from one to

A car contains metal which is a good conductor of heat. This computer image shows the temperature of the different parts of a car which has just stopped. The white areas are the hottest and include the bonnet over the engine and the hub caps.

Would food cook more quickly in a glass dish or one made from metal?

another. Metals are good conductors of heat, so they are used in saucepans. Insulators are poor conductors of heat. Air is a really good insulator and so are materials that contain many air spaces, for example glass, wool and cotton.

Convection

What type of insulators are used in your home?

A hot radiator can quickly warm a room. First it heats the air above the radiator. As the molecules in the air gain heat energy they move more rapidly. The air becomes less dense or lighter and begins to rise. As the warm air rises, cool air is drawn towards the radiator and this gets warmed. The result is a circulation of air called a convection current, which quickly carries the heat around the room. Many birds make use of natural convection currents, for example pelicans and vultures. The currents are called thermals and they are formed when warm air rises up from the ground. The birds circle upwards within the thermal and then glide down to the ground again, covering great distances.

These pelicans are using thermals to rise high above the Rift Valley in Kenya

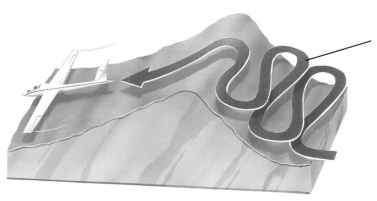

current of warm air

Gliders use thermals, too. The glider spirals up on a thermal and then slowly glides down again.

Radiation

 Ten people dancing in a room will give off more heat energy than a gas fire.

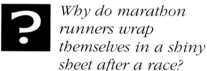 *Why do marathon runners wrap themselves in a shiny sheet after a race?*

Hot objects give out invisible light and heat energy called infrared. The infrared heat from the sun travels through space and warms the Earth. An electric fire will give out radiated heat too. Radiated heat travels in straight lines. If you sit in front of the fire you feel the heat on your face but your back will feel cold. A fire which gives out radiant heat only warms a small part of a room. A radiator is more effective because it heats by convection.

The colour of a surface affects the amount of heat energy that is absorbed. Dark colours absorb more heat than light colours. In winter we wear darker colours, but in summer whites and pale colours are more comfortable because they reflect more of the heat. Shiny or polished surfaces absorb the least heat because they reflect most of the radiant heat.

EXPERIMENT

Coloured surfaces

Some colours are better at absorbing heat than others. You will need four jam jars with lids, black, red and white paint, a paint brush, some Plasticine, scissors, a long thermometer and some water. You may need to ask an adult to help you with the scissors.

1 Using the ends of the scissors, make a hole in the centre of each of the lids. It should be large enough to allow the thermometer through. Paint the outside of three of the jam jars in a different colour and leave the fourth one unpainted.
2 Fill each jar with cold water and replace the lid.
3 Use a small piece of Plasticine to block up the hole in the lid.
4 Place the four jars in a warm place, such as a sunny window ledge or above a radiator.
5 After 10 minutes remove the Plasticine and take the temperature of the water in each of the jars.
Which jar warmed up the quickest?

Why are houses in hot countries often painted white?

Marathon runners in thermal wraps at the end of a race.

The space shuttle is covered in shiny tiles which help to reflect heat as the shuttle re-enters the Earth's atmosphere.

Shape and size

Key words
Conduction the transfer of heat from one molecule to another as they bump into each other.
Convection the transfer of heat by the movement of the heated molecules themselves.
Radiation the giving out of heat by a hot object.

The shape and size of an object affects heat loss. If a large and a small block of ice are placed in the sun the smaller block will melt more quickly than the large one. But a small block of rock would heat up more quickly than a large one. Small objects have a large surface area compared to their volume so they lose or gain heat more quickly. This affects the shape of animals. Polar animals are often large with a small surface area so they lose heat slowly.

Keeping warm

Heat is needed by all living things. Animals living in the coldest parts of the world have to conserve their body heat to survive. If their cells freeze they will burst open, just as water in a frozen pipe will expand and crack the pipe. So these animals have developed very effective ways of conserving heat. People who live or work in the polar regions or in deep water have to survive the cold conditions too. They make use of the latest designs in clothing and energy-saving equipment.

Divers may wear a dry suit to stay warm in cold water. A layer of air between the skin and the suit reduces the heat loss.

Surviving the cold

The mountain goat of the Rockies survives the severe winter with temperatures that fall to

Mountain goats have a thick coat which reduces heat loss. Human mountaineers wear clothing made of the latest insulating materials to stay warm.

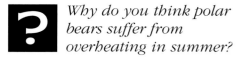

Why do you think polar bears suffer from overheating in summer?

-50 °C. It has a long shaggy white coat. The thick fur contains a lot of air spaces that insulate the animal. Polar bears also have a thick coat. Beneath their fur their skin is black and this helps to absorb as much heat as possible. Their insulation is so good that their bodies give off no heat at all.

The Emperor penguin is the only animal that is able to survive the extreme cold of the Antarctic winter. The adult penguins huddle together on the ice to keep warm. As they huddle they slowly shift position, each taking turns to stand on the outside. Seals are found in the icy polar waters. They have a thick insulating layer of fat beneath the skin called blubber, which prevents heat loss.

Icefish live in the freezing waters of the North Atlantic. They make their own antifreeze to stop their cells from freezing. Scientists are hoping to be able to insert a gene into bacteria

Emperor penguins have long feathers which create a thick insulating layer. Unlike other birds their feathers extend down their legs to give even more insulation.

EXPERIMENT

Huddling

Penguins huddle together to save heat. You can test this out for yourself. You will need 10 small jam jars, some warm water and a thermometer.

1 Group the jars together so that they are touching each other in a huddle.

2 Fill the jam jars with warm water to within 2 cm of the top.

3 Take the temperature of the water in all the jam jars.

4 After 20 minutes take the temperature again. Which jam jars cooled down more quickly?

Antifreeze stops the water in a car radiator from freezing.

The icefish can live in very cold water because its cells can make a natural antifreeze.

that will allow them to make their own antifreeze. The bacterial antifreeze could be made in large quantities for use on icy roads and on crops. Man-made antifreeze is used in the cooling systems of cars to stop the water freezing during cold weather. If the water was allowed to freeze it would expand and crack the car's radiator or cooling pipes.

Insulation

Insulation reduces heat loss so it is important in cold climates. The Inuit people live in the Arctic. Their traditional clothing is made from the skin of seals, polar bears and caribou. Now there are artificial fibres that are just as good as fur and feathers. Finely spun polyester is soft and light. It traps air which acts as an insulator.

Houses need to be insulated too. A well insulated house will cost less to heat and help to conserve our dwindling supply of fossil fuels. New houses are given an energy rating which tells the owner how well the house retains heat. Double glazing, roof and cavity-wall insulation and draught excluders all reduce heat loss.

Reptiles, fish and amphibians are ectothermic. This means that their bodies gain all their heat from the environment. Their

A thick layer of insulation in the loft can stop a lot of heat energy escaping through the roof.

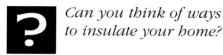

Can you think of ways to insulate your home?

Mountain lizards from Peru can warm up their bodies from -2°C to over 30 °C in just one hour.

The collared lizard basks in the sun to absorb heat energy.

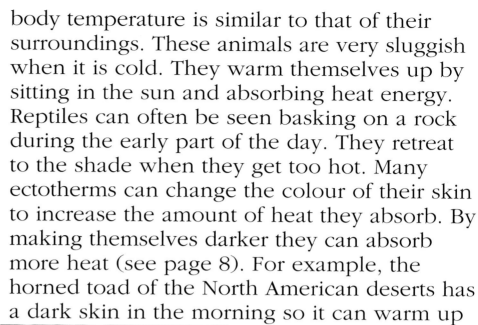

body temperature is similar to that of their surroundings. These animals are very sluggish when it is cold. They warm themselves up by sitting in the sun and absorbing heat energy. Reptiles can often be seen basking on a rock during the early part of the day. They retreat to the shade when they get too hot. Many ectotherms can change the colour of their skin to increase the amount of heat they absorb. By making themselves darker they can absorb more heat (see page 8). For example, the horned toad of the North American deserts has a dark skin in the morning so it can warm up quickly. But as the day gets hotter the skin becomes lighter and reflects more heat. This way the toad can stay in the sun for longer without overheating. Some reptiles try to maximise the amount of their skin that is in the sun by spreading their legs and flattening their body.

Heat exchangers

All mammals and birds are endothermic. This means that their body temperature remains the same regardless of the temperature of their surroundings. A human's body

EXPERIMENT

Insulation

Find out which materials make good insulators. You will need four small jam jars, a thermometer, some Plasticine, warm water, and a selection of insulating materials, such as feathers, cotton wool, newspaper and aluminium foil.

1 Make a hole in each of the lids large enough for your thermometer. You may need to ask an adult to help you.

2 Wrap a layer of insulating material around three of the jam jars, making sure you have enough to cover the lids as well. Leave one jam jar with no insulation at all.

3 Carefully fill each jar three-quarters full of warm water. Screw the lid in place. Make a note of the temperature of the water in each jar. Then cover the lid with the insulating material and place a knob of Plasticine over the hole.

4 Leave the jam jars for 10 minutes and take the temperature of the water in each jar.

Which was the best insulator?

temperature will be 37°C even if they are in the tropics or in the Arctic. Whales live in water a few degrees above freezing point (0°C) so they cannot afford to lose heat. They have a thick layer of blubber under their skin except on their flippers. The flippers have a large surface area, a lot of blood vessels and little insulation. This means whales could lose body heat through their flippers. The blood vessels are arranged in such a way that prevents heat loss. The blood vessel that carries warm blood from the body to the flipper is

This humpback whale has heat exchangers in its flipper so that it does not lose heat to the cold water.

The heat exchangers in the flippers of whales and in condensing boilers both save heat energy.

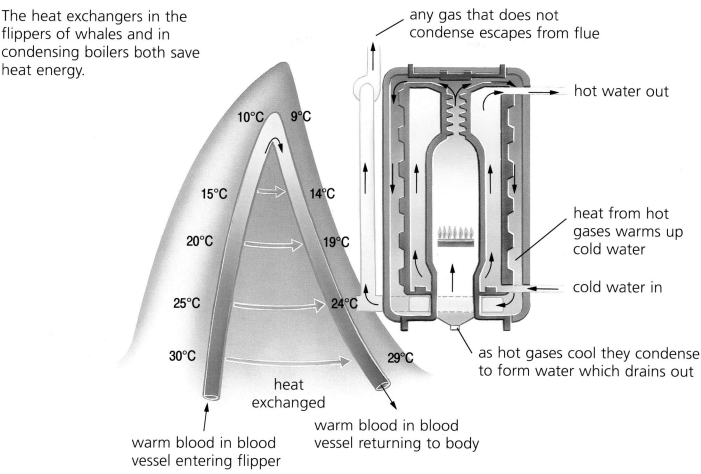

any gas that does not condense escapes from flue

hot water out

heat from hot gases warms up cold water

cold water in

as hot gases cool they condense to form water which drains out

10°C 9°C

15°C 14°C

20°C 19°C

25°C 24°C

30°C 29°C

heat exchanged

warm blood in blood vessel returning to body

warm blood in blood vessel entering flipper

completely surrounded by vessels that carry cold blood out of the flipper. As the warm blood flows into the flipper it loses its heat to the cold blood. By the time this blood has reached the outside of the flipper it is cold and no heat is lost. This system is called a heat exchanger.

A similar system is found in new boilers. The burning fuel releases heat that is used to heat the water flowing through pipes in the boiler. But hot waste gases are also produced. Normally these are carried away to the outside by the flue, wasting the heat energy. The latest boilers make better use of the waste gases. They are called condensing boilers. As the hot waste gases are taken away from the boiler they pass close to pipes containing cold water. The hot gases get cooler as the water gets warmer.

Key words
Endotherm an animal whose body temperature remains the same regardless of the changes in the temperature of its surroundings.
Ectotherm an animal that relies on heat from its surroundings to warm its body.
Insulation a layer of material or air that keeps in heat.

Keeping cool

Biological washing powders contain enzymes. Why do these powders work best with low temperatures?

There are many reasons why living organisms need to keep cool. One of the most important is to keep chemicals called enzymes at their ideal temperature. Enzymes are chemicals which speed up reactions in cells. Your saliva contains enzymes which break down starch into sugar. This reaction only takes a few seconds. But without the enzyme it would take several hours. Enzymes are affected by temperature. Too high a temperature and the enzyme is destroyed, too low and the enzyme is slowed down, eventually becoming inactive. So it is important that the body is kept at the right temperature.

Evaporation

Living organisms and machines all use similar methods for keeping cool. You have already read how heat can be lost by conduction, convection, and radiation (see pages 6-8), but heat can be lost by evaporation too. Evaporation occurs when a liquid turns into a gas. For example, when water boils at 100 °C steam is seen rising from the surface of the water. The water has been changed from liquid to a gas – water vapour. But water does not have to be boiling for evaporation to occur. Water

Dogs open their mouths and pant to keep cool.

Crocodiles keep cool by opening their mouths so water can evaporate.

will evaporate from clothes on a washing line or from puddles on the ground.

Evaporation needs heat energy. The heat energy makes the molecules in the water move faster. Molecules moving near the surface of the water may escape and form a vapour. The heat energy is taken from the water itself. As evaporation takes place the water becomes cooler.

Many animals use evaporation to cool down. Humans produce a liquid called sweat from their sweat glands in the skin.

African elephants use their large ears like fans.

If you place perfume on your skin it quickly evaporates. Why does you skin feel cool?

A person in a hot desert could evaporate 1.5 litres of sweat each hour. If he or she had no water to drink they could die of dehydration within 12 hours.

Heat energy in the skin is used to turn the sweat into vapour. This cools the skin. Cattle, camels and horses can sweat, but other mammals such as cats and dogs cannot. They pant or lick themselves instead. Panting helps water to evaporate from the warm surfaces of the mouth and tongue. Cats lick their fur and as the water evaporates it cools their body. Crocodiles keep cool by gaping. They open their huge mouth to allow water to evaporate.

The blood can be cooled as it passes through the skin. When you get hot your skin becomes red and flushed. This is because

If the hive gets too hot bees fan their wings to create cooling currents of air.

more blood is flowing near the surface of the skin so more heat can be lost.

Animals that live in hot, tropical climates often have large ears and long, thin limbs. This gives a larger surface area to lose heat. The bat-eared fox has extra large ears with lots of blood vessels and these radiate heat into the surroundings. Elephants lose heat through their ears too. They will flap their ears to increase the heat loss.

Bees have to control the temperature inside their hive. In summer its temperature tends to stay around 35°C, which is ideal for young bee larvae. If it gets too hot the bees spread water droplets in the hive and as the water evaporates it cools the air. The bees may fan their wings to create cooling currents. If the temperature falls the bees huddle together to keep warm.

Refrigerators

 Why are the coils at the back of a refrigerator warm?

The food in this refrigerator is kept cool by evaporation.

Refrigerators are used to keep food cool so it stays fresh for longer. The cooling process involves evaporation and a coolant. The coolant is a liquid that easily evaporates into a vapour. When this happens the coolant takes up heat. When it condenses back to a liquid it gives out heat. The coolant is placed in a coiled tube that runs from the inside to the back of the refrigerator. When the coolant passes along the tube

During the Expo 92 exhibition in Spain water droplets were sprayed into the air. They evaporated and cooled the air.

The trees in this Hong Kong park help to cool the air.

inside the refrigerator it evaporates and this takes up heat from the air and cools it. When the coolant passes through the coils at the back of the refrigerator it condenses back to a liquid, releasing heat. Air conditioning systems work in a similar way, cooling the inside of a building.

Water evaporates from the surfaces of plant leaves. This is called transpiration. The main role of transpiration is not to cool the plant, but it does have a use for people! When you walk under trees on a hot day the air is much cooler under the trees than in the open. The plant's transpiration has cooled the air. City planners now make better use of trees as natural air conditioners.

Key words
Evaporation the change from liquid water to water vapour, using heat energy.
Transpiration the evaporation of water from the leaves of plants.

Energy from the sun

The sun pumps out vast amounts of light and heat energy. This solar energy is produced by the nuclear reactions taking place inside the sun. Much of the light and heat energy that reaches the Earth is reflected by our atmosphere back into space. Only a tiny fraction eventually reaches the surface of the planet, but this is enough to support life. The amount of solar energy reaching the surface varies, with the tropics receiving more energy than the poles.

Solar cells and leaves both use energy from the sun.

Plants and light energy

The leaves of these rainforest trees are pointed towards the sun to trap the maximum amount of sunlight.

Green plants make the greatest use of light energy, which they use to make food. This food is then used by animals, so plants are at the bottom of the food chains. Without plants, animals would not survive.

The leaves of the plant are designed to trap as much light as possible. They are flat, thin and have a large surface area. The light energy is converted to chemical energy in a process called photosynthesis. This is a complex process but it can be summarised in one equation :

light + carbon dioxide + water = food + oxygen

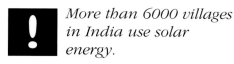

More than 6000 villages in India use solar energy.

In less that one hour, the Earth receives energy from the sun that is equivalent to the total energy gained form all other sources in an entire year.

What type of foods contain starch?

Plants can use light energy because their leaves contain a green pigment called chlorophyll. When sunlight falls on the chlorophyll it absorbs the light energy which is then used to fuel the process of changing carbon dioxide (a gas in air) and water into sugar. The sugar may be used as an energy source for growth or it may be changed to starch for storage in the roots. Oxygen is a very important product of photosynthesis. It passes out of the leaf into the air to be used by animals.

Capturing solar energy

In the sunnier parts of the world sunlight is an important source of energy. It can be used to heat water or make electricity in remote places where normal electricity is not available, for example to provide hot water in Nepal and electricity for communications equipment in East Africa.

A solar panel has a large, flat surface

This remote telecom relay station in Australia is powered by solar energy.

which absorbs the heat energy of the sun and uses it to heat water or air. The simplest type solar panel has a black plate which is good at absorbing heat. As water flows across the plate in pipes it absorbs the heat.

Some houses are built with glass walls on their south side. The glass wall acts like a greenhouse, allowing the heat and light into the house. This heats up the air inside the building. At night a black curtain is put across the glass wall to stop the heat energy escaping.

The glass wall of this house in Wales lets in sunlight, which helps to heat the air within the house.

Solar panels capture solar energy to heat water, but this has limited uses. Solar or photovoltaic cells can change light into electrical energy. You may have seen these in calculators. These cells are made from thin layers of a material called a semiconductor. When the sunlight strikes the cell light, energy is changed into electricity. More light shining on a cell produces more electricity.

Unfortunately there is no easy way of storing the electricity produced by solar cells. If it is not used, it is wasted. But soon it may be possible for houses with solar cells to have special connections to the electricity supply. If the solar cells do not make enough electricity, the house takes electricity from the main supply. But if the cells produce surplus electricity this can be fed into the supply.

In summer these solar panels absorb heat energy, which is used to heat water.

Thousands of mirrors on this solar power station in France reflect sunlight onto the central tower, where the heat energy is used to make steam.

! *Solar power is not a new discovery – 3000 years ago a palace in Turkey was warmed using water heated by the sun.*

! *If solar panels covered just 0.1 per cent of the Mojave Desert they could supply Los Angeles with all its electricity.*

Key words
Photosynthesis the process of making sugar using light energy in green plants.
Solar cell a device that can convert light energy into electricity.
Solar panel a device that uses heat energy from the sun to heat water.

Solar power stations

The first solar power stations consisted of thousands of solar panels. They heated up water which was pumped to a central heat exchanger, where steam was produced. The steam is used to produce electricity. Newer solar power stations have thousands of mirrors which reflect the sunlight onto the top of a central power collection tower. Then the heat energy is absorbed by black pipes which contain liquid sodium. This will then heat water to make steam.

Changing energy

Animals have to be able to unlock the energy found in food and change it to a form of energy that their bodies can use.

Energy can be changed from one form to another. For example, from chemical to movement energy. One of the most useful forms of energy that we use every day is electrical energy. It provides lighting and heating, and it powers our radios and televisions. We can make electricity by burning fuels, or using the energy of sunlight, wind and waves. Animals too, can generate their own electricity.

Electricity

When you use a hair dryer, 20 million million million electrons pass along the wire every second.

Tiny particles called electrons can be made to move and form an electric current. An electric current needs a path or circuit to flow along, such as a copper wire, and a force to push the current along the wire, for example a battery. When the circuit is switched on, the battery produces a force which pushes on the nearest electrons. These electrons move a short distance and bump into other electrons, which bump into others. This way the current passes along the circuit.

Conductors and insulators

Conductors are substances which allow a current of electricity to flow through them. The best conductors are metals such as gold and copper. Materials which do not allow electricity to pass through them are called insulators. An electricity cable is encased in a plastic sleeve which acts as an insulator. It allows the cable

Static electricity has caused the hairs on this wig to stand up. Static electricity is produced when two objects are rubbed together.

to be touched, protecting the person from the electric current inside the wire.

EXPERIMENT

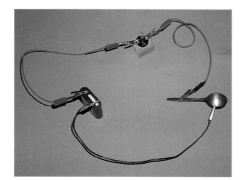

Find out which household items are conductors and which are insulators.

You will need a 4.5V battery (as found in a torch or radio), three electrical leads, a small light bulb and holder and a selection of items to test from the kitchen, such as scissors, plastic and metal spoons, baking trays, aluminium foil.
1 First connect the three wires, battery and bulb in a circuit. If everything is in the right place the light bulb will light up.
2 Insert the test item into the circuit (as shown in the photograph). If it is a conductor the light bulb will come on. If it is an insulator the light bulb will remain off.

Electromagnetism

The cooling tower of a power station will cool the hot steam so that it condenses back into water which can be reused.

Magnets create an electric current when they are moved into a coil of wire. Inside the generators of power stations are huge magnets placed inside a coil of wires. As the coils spin they create an electric current. The amount of electricity produced can be increased by adding more coils to the wire and spinning it faster. The power station burns a fuel such as oil or coal to release heat energy. This is used to heat water and produce steam. Steam is the force used to turn the turbines which spin the coils (see page 23).

Alternative energy sources

Water stored in the reservoir behind the dam is used to spin the turbines. When the turbines spin, their movement energy is changed into electrical energy.

Moving water is an important source of energy. In the past, flowing water was used by mills to spin water wheels that would turn a millstone. The millstone would grind grain into flour.

Why should we use renewable sources of energy, such as wind and water, rather than oil and coal?

Wind farms, such as this one in California, are built in mountain passes and on hillside where the wind blows all year round.

Today, fast-flowing water is used to generate electricity. Rivers are dammed to create a lake or reservoir of water. Water is allowed to fall through pipes in the dam. The energy of the falling water is used to drive a turbine which, in turn, spins the electromagnet to make electricity. A lot of hydroelectricity can be made in places where there are many fast flowing rivers, for example Norway and Sweden. Small dams can be built across streams and rivers where a drop in height of just one metre is enough to produce electricity for a whole village. However, damming rivers can create environmental problems because a reservoir will flood a lot of land and the natural flow of the river has been controlled.

Windmills have been built in windy places for hundreds of years. They were used to turn millstones or pump water. Today modern wind generators are used to make electricity. The wind generators are grouped together to form wind farms. Wind and water energy are renewable forms of energy, and unlike fossil fuels, they will not run out (see page 21-23 on solar energy).

EXPERIMENT

Making electricity

See how you can produce electricity using a magnet. You will need a length of wire, crocodile clips, a bar magnet, a thick pencil or piece of wood dowel, and an ammeter for measuring the current of electricity.

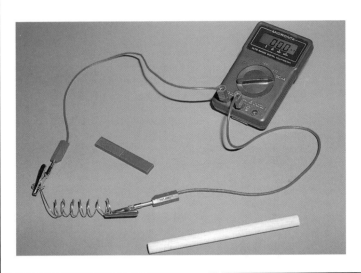

1 Wrap the wire around the pencil or dowel to make a coil with 8-10 turns. Make sure the magnet can fit inside the coil. If it is too small use several pencils or a thicker piece of dowel.

2 Clip the ends of the wire coil to the ammeter.

3 Move the magnet in and out of the coil. Watch the ammeter while you do this. Does the ammeter show a current?

Animals and electricity

The South American electric eel produces electric shocks strong enough to kill other fish and even human beings.

The elephant trunk fish from West Africa can produce electric shocks.

Some fish, such as the electric eel, have developed the ability to produce strong electric shocks. These fish use the electric shocks to scare away predators. The fish can also learn about its environment using weak electrical discharges. It can tell whether something in its surroundings is an insulator or a conductor such as another animal. The discharges also help the animal to finds its way around in murky water. Salt water is a much better conductor of electricity than fresh water.

Many animals are very sensitive to electrical currents in the water. The shark has special sense organs in its skin called electroreceptors.

The duck-billed platypus uses electroreceptors in its bill to find shrimps on the river bed.

These receptors are used to hunt prey animals. They can detect the electrical activity produced when animals use their muscles.

Energy efficiency

A filament light bulb is not very efficient as only 3 per cent of the electrical energy is converted into light. Cows waste a lot of energy when they graze grass. They do not eat dead leaves and roots.

This diagram shows what happens to the chemical energy in food. Only a small amount will be used to do work. More than half is lost as heat energy.

heat energy

chemical energy in body wastes

growth and repair

work e.g. moving muscles

chemical energy in food

When electrical energy is changed into light energy in a light bulb, heat energy is also released. The heat is unwanted and represents wasted energy. It would be much more efficient if all the electrical energy became light energy. But few energy changes are 100 per cent efficient. One of the most efficient is an electric fire. Some batteries are almost 90 per cent efficient, but the car engine is only 25 per cent efficient. This means that for every litre of petrol burnt by the engine, only 25 per cent of the chemical energy locked in the fuel is changed into movement energy. The rest is changed to heat.

Animals are not very efficient. When a cow eats grass, only 10-20 per cent of the energy locked up in the grass is taken up and built in the cells of the cow. The rest is wasted, because the cow only eats the fresh green leaves of the grass, not the dead

Energy losses in a food chain

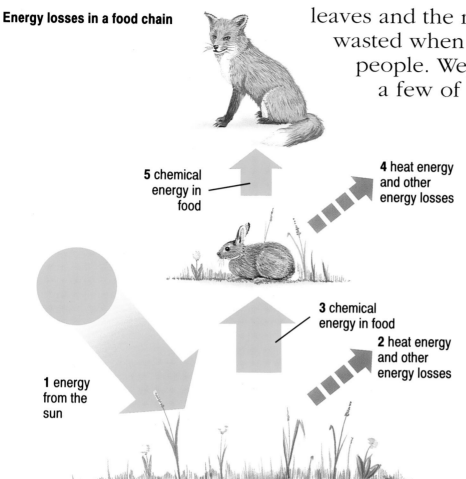

5 chemical energy in food

4 heat energy and other energy losses

3 chemical energy in food

2 heat energy and other energy losses

1 energy from the sun

leaves and the roots. More energy is wasted when cows are eaten by people. We only eat the muscle and a few of the organs. The rest of the cow is wasted. If people ate a mostly vegetarian diet, crops would be used to feed people rather than animals such as cows and sheep.

 Why is it more energy efficient to eat vegetables than meat?

 In a typical industrialised country each year power stations release enough waste heat to keep all the homes in the country warm!

In many developing countries people eat very little meat. They have a vegetarian diet with rice or maize, vegetables and fruit.

Key words
Conductor a substance that allows electric currents to flow through it
Electron a tiny particle that has a negative charge.
Insulator a substance that does not allow electric currents to flow through it.

Dry batteries store chemical energy, which is changed to electrical energy to power torches, radios and toys.

These charcoal briquettes are made from wood. They contain chemical energy which is changed into heat energy.

Storing energy

Every day we all rely on stored chemical energy in fossil fuels and batteries. The fossil fuels power our cars and heat our homes. The energy stored in a battery can be used to produce an electrical current that powers a radio or torch. Animals store energy too, in the form of fat, while plants can store starch.

Fossil fuels

Oil, coal, gas and peat are all fossil fuels. The stored energy they contain is released when the fuel is burnt in air. They are called fossil fuels because they have been made from the fossilised remains of plants and animals that lived millions of years ago. For example, oil and gas are made from the remains of marine animals. When these animals died they sank to the sea floor where they were buried under mud. Over a long period of time a thick layer of mud formed over the dead bodies. The immense weight of the mud crushed the dead bodies, which turned into a liquid. Millions of years later this liquid is extracted as oil.

Coal is made from the buried remains of plants. In the first stage of the coal-making process the plant remains become peat. As the peat becomes buried under more layers of dead plants and mud it is squashed, making it harder. It changes slowly to coal.

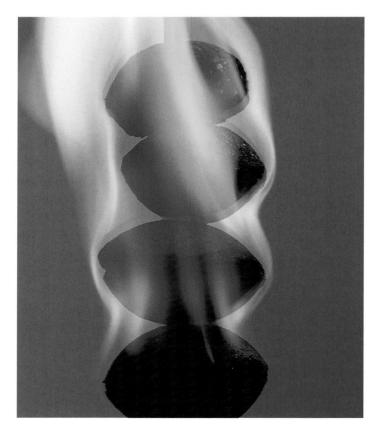

Battery power

A simple dry cell battery

central electrode of carbon

zinc casing forms the second electrode

gel of ammonium chloride

Batteries store chemical energy. When the battery is used, its stored chemical energy is changed to electrical energy. There are many different types of battery, but they all work in the same way. The most common form is the dry battery. The dry battery has two electrodes, one made from zinc and the other from carbon, with a gel filling the space between them (see diagram on left). The battery acts like an electron pump. When the battery is connected to an electrical circuit, a chemical reaction takes place in the liquid and this produces electrons. Electrons are pumped from the negative terminal of the battery, creating a current. The battery continues to produce an electric current until all the chemicals are used up. Then the battery is said to be flat. Some dry batteries can be recharged by a passing a small electric current through the battery for several hours. By joining up a number of batteries, a larger electric force, or voltage, can be produced. Cars use a 12V battery made up of six smaller batteries. They have lead electrodes and contain an acid solution. This type of battery is called a lead-acid battery and can be recharged several times.

These lead-acid batteries are flat. They contain acids so they must be disposed of carefully.

! *Some dry batteries can be recharged up to 700 times.*

EXPERIMENT

A natural battery

See how you can use a lemon as a battery! You will need a lemon, some copper wire, a 1.5V light bulb with holder, a strip of zinc, a strip of thin copper metal. You should be able to buy these metals from an ironmonger or a workshop.

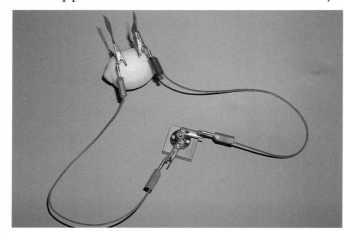

1. Cut two parallel slits on the top of the lemon about 2 cm apart. Push the zinc strip into one slit and the copper strip into the other.

2. Using the copper wire, connect the zinc strip to one terminal of the light bulb holder and the copper strip to the other. Now you should have a complete circuit and the light bulb should glow.

Unfortunately your battery will not last very long, but it is more fun than a real battery! You could try out different vegetables and fruits, for example a potato.

Biomass

Compost heaps are very warm inside. Where does the heat come from?

Wood can be grown as a source of renewable fuel. After the harvest, new trees can be planted for the future. Willow and birch are

In a coppiced wood the trees are cut to ground level. New shoots appear from the cut stump and can be harvested in about 10 years.

It is estimated that, in the USA, the energy that could be generated from burning biomass, including garden waste, wood and waste paper, would equal the energy released by 200 nuclear power plants.

fast-growing trees and can be harvested in just a few years. It's not just wood that can be used. Plant twigs, leaves, straw and even unwanted vegetable scraps can be used to generate energy. Plant material used in this way is called biomass. Instead of burning the biomass, the plant material can be allowed to rot in special containers. As it rots it releases a gas called methane, which can be collected and used as a fuel.

Natural storage

This onion has just started to grow. The new green leaves use the energy stored in the bulb for growth.

Animals and plants store energy for future use. Plants store starch in their roots or in tubers or bulbs. This starch is used to fuel their spring growth. Seeds also contain starch which is used by the young seedling.

Starch is an important energy-rich food for many animals, including humans. When an animal eats too much food the excess energy can be converted to fat and stored.

▷ Pulses are the seeds of the pea family – peas, beans, lentils. They are an important source of starch and protein in our diet.

The dormouse hibernates during the winter.

Some small mammals eat a lot of food in autumn and get very fat, ready for their long winter sleep. This is called hibernation. During hibernation the beating of their heart slows down and their body temperature falls. They use their energy stores very slowly so they last all winter.

Many mammals shiver when they get cold. This releases heat. But new-born babies, including

EXPERIMENT

Find out which foods contain starch.

You will need some iodine (this an be obtained from a chemist), a selection of foods such as potato, bread, biscuit, carrot, cheese, onion, a mortar and pestle, a knife, and a small clear plastic or glass container.
Make sure you ask an adult to help.

1 Take one of the food samples and chop it into small pieces with the knife. Place the food in the mortar and grind it up with some water.

2 Leave the food and water mix to settle for a few minutes and then pour off the liquid into the container.

3 Add a few drops of iodine to the liquid in the container. If starch is present the liquid will turn blue-black. If there is no starch the liquid will turn the colour of the iodine.

4 Try this out on all your food samples.

The body temperature of a hibernating mammal may fall as low as 3°C.

human babies, cannot shiver. So they are kept warm by the heat of their surroundings and by the heat released from a special fat in their bodies. They have patches of brown fat which can release far more heat than normal fat.

Deep heat stores

Geothermal energy sources provide energy for 3 million homes in the USA

The Earth is a huge energy store. Below the surface of the Earth the rocks are hot. This heat energy is called geothermal energy and it can be used to heat water. By drilling pipes deep into the hot rock water can be pumped down into the rock. The water is heated and then pumped back to the surface. This can then be used to heat homes or to produce steam in power stations.

This geothermal power station in Iceland uses heat energy stored deep in the ground.

Key words
Battery a device that stores chemical energy which can be used to produce an electric current.
Fossil fuel a type of fuel made from the remains of plants and animals that died millions of years ago.

Engines

Engines are machines that change one form of energy into another, for example heat into movement energy. Most people think of engines as being man-made, but living organisms are natural engines. Our bodies convert chemical energy in food into other forms, including movement energy.

A car engine converts chemical energy into movement energy. The cyclist is also an engine. Her body converts chemical energy into movement energy, which is used to turn the wheels.

Engines turn the chemical energy locked up in fuel into movement energy. The chemical substances which make up the fuels release energy when they are burnt in air. This is called combustion. The heat energy produced from burning fuel is changed into movement energy, which makes the wheels turn. A similar process takes place in cells when sugars are carefully broken down in the presence of air to release energy.

Engines

Cars and some planes have an internal combustion engine. The fuel is mixed with air and burnt in closed cylinders within the engine. This type of engine is made of two parts bolted together. The first is the cylinder head which contains the combustion chamber and the camshaft. The second is the cylinder block which contains the crankshaft. Petrol and air are drawn into the combustion chamber. A spark from the spark plug ignites

How a four-stroke combustion engine works

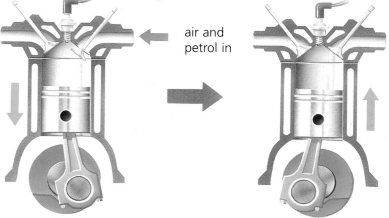

air and petrol in

Fuel intake: the piston moves down and the valves are open. Petrol and air enter the combustion chamber.

Compression: the valves are closed and the piston rises, pressing on the mixture.

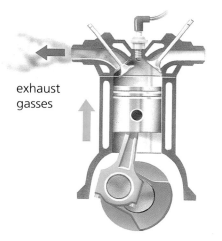

exhaust gasses

Exhaust: the piston rises and forces the gases out through the exhaust.

Combustion: the mixture is ignited by a spark from the spark plugs. The exploding gases expand and force the piston down.

Electric cars are quiet and less polluting, but the battery is large and heavy.

the mix. As it explodes it forces the piston down. The piston is connected to the crankshaft. The crankshaft is connected to the wheels via the gear box. When the piston moves down it forces the crankshaft to rotate and this spins the wheel.

Unfortunately, combustion engines are not very efficient, especially at low speeds. Only a quarter of the chemical energy in the fuel is changed to useful energy. The rest is lost as heat.

Electric engines are quiet, work well at low speeds and most importantly, do not produce air pollution. However, their batteries are heavy and cannot store as much energy as a fuel tank, so their range is limited. But they may become popular in cities.

Electric engines

A simple electric motor
When the battery is connected, an electric current flows through the coil of wire. The current produces a force that turns the coil and the wooden block.

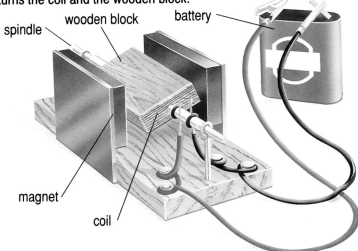

spindle
wooden block
battery
magnet
coil

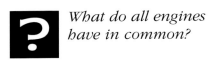

What do all engines have in common?

If a magnet is placed close to a length of wire and a current is passed along the wire, both the magnet and wire try to move apart. This movement is called the motor effect. Electric motors have very many uses and are found in toys and electric vehicles. More movement can be produced if the wire is coiled.

Sometimes a magnet is placed inside the coil to make the coil into an electromagnet, producing a more efficient motor. But the spinning coil of the electromagnet in a motor is moved by electricity, while the spinning coil in a generator produces electricity.

Natural engines

Respiration in a cell

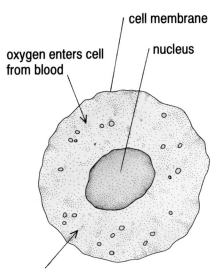

cell membrane
nucleus
oxygen enters cell from blood
glucose enters cell from blood

There is an engine that is quiet, works well at low speed, uses renewable fuel and produces little pollution – the human body. But it cannot move very heavy loads and it gets tired!

Food is fuel to our bodies. The food is digested in the gut and then absorbed through the gut wall into the blood stream. One of these foods is glucose, a type of simple sugar. It is taken up by cells which need energy, especially liver and muscle cells. Once in the cell, the glucose is broken down into smaller substances in a process called respiration. This takes place as a series of small steps, so that only a small amount of energy is released at

EXPERIMENT

Respiration and heat energy

Find out how much heat energy is released by respiration. You will need a small thermos flask, cotton wool, a long thermometer, and 200g of dried peas.

1 Place the peas in a container and cover them with water. Allow them to soak for one day. They will start to germinate.

2 Half fill the thermos flask with peas. Place a piece of cotton wool in the neck of the flask.

3 Gently push the thermometer into the middle of the flask and read off the temperature. Remove the thermometer.

4 Support the flask upside down and leave for a week. (Heat will rise so by turning the flask upside down the heat cannot escape). Take another thermometer reading. By how much has the temperature increased?

 Which parts of your body release each of the following – sound energy, movement energy and heat energy?

one time. The final products are carbon dioxide and water.

There are two types of respiration. One uses oxygen and is called aerobic respiration. The other does not need oxygen and is called anaerobic respiration.

During a sprint race an athlete (below) may not breathe in enough oxygen so she has to respire anaerobically for a short time until she 'gets her breath back'. Beer and wine making relies on yeast cells (right) respiring anaerobically to produce alcohol.

Key words
Combustion a process which releases energy when a chemical is burnt in air.
Respiration a process which releases energy from foods.

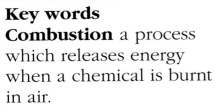

Our rubbish is a useful source of energy. It could be used as a fuel in power stations.

The future

Fossil fuels represent millions of years of stored sunshine. They are a convenient source of stored energy, but they are being used up faster than they are being formed. Eventually they will run out. People have to make better use of renewable sources of energy. Soon cars may run on alternative fuels such as propane and hydrogen. Power stations may be able to burn more types of fuel, for example animal slurry (similar to sewage), domestic refuse and wood.

Nuclear power stations use uranium metal as their source of fuel. Uranium rods are placed in a reactor and tiny particles called neutrons are fired at the uranium. This causes the large uranium atoms to split and release large amounts of energy. Unfortunately this produces radioactive waste which is long-

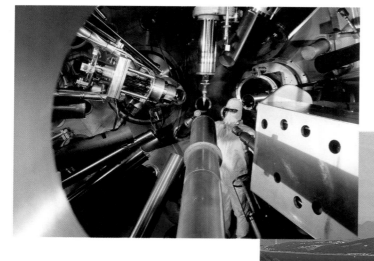

Today's nuclear power stations (right) split the atom to release energy. Tomorrow's nuclear power may be produced by joining atoms. The Nova laser (above) is used to start a nuclear fusion reaction.

lived and harmful to living organisms. It is possible that another nuclear reaction, called nuclear fusion, may offer hope. Small atoms are fused or joined together to make a larger atom, and heat energy is released. At the moment the reaction will only work at extremely high temperatures. But as technology makes advances this form of nuclear energy may become possible.

The arctic avens is a small plant with a yellow cup-shaped flower found in the Arctic. Even in summer the Arctic temperatures are cold. The shape of the flower is designed to reflect the sunlight into the middle of the flower, where the reproductive parts are found. This raises the temperature by 10 °C. The extra warmth attracts insects which pollinate the flower. The latest solar water heaters have a similar shape. They have cup-shaped mirrors that focus the sunlight on one exact spot. This makes the heaters far more efficient.

Energy is essential for life. The world's energy needs are increasing but our supply of fossil fuels is falling. If our energy-hungry lifestyle is to continue we will have to find new ways of generating and using energy.

The cup-shaped flower of the arctic avens is ideally shaped to reflect sunlight into the middle of the flower. The latest designs of solar water heater use a similar shape.

Glossary

antifreeze a substance that stops a liquid from freezing

biomass a living mass of organisms, for example the mass of pond weed in a pond.

chlorophyll the green pigment found in plants

coolant a substance, often a liquid which cools a machine by removing the heat energy

coppicing the cutting of tree trunks at ground level and allowing the shoots to regrow

enzyme a substance found in living cells which speeds up chemical reactions

flue a vent through which gases can escape

force a push or pull

gene a unit of inheritance, passed on from parent to offspring.

geothermal a source of heat from the ground

infrared heat radiation invisible light given out by hot objects

molecule a group of atoms bonded together

neutron a tiny particle with neutral charge found in the nucleus of an atom

protein a large molecule made form many amino acids, found in living organisms

reservoir a large artificial store of water or lake, found behind a dam

semi conductor a material that only partially conducts electricity

static electricity form of electricity which does not move and which is created by an attraction between electrically charged objects

vapour a gas

vibrate a forward and backward motion

Index